Bears

by:
Kason Anari

Published by:

Bears

Copyright 2020 by North Star Success Inc.

For permission requests and bulk orders, please contact support@northstarsuccess.com.

Kason Anari is hereby identified as author of this work in accordance with Section 77 of the Copyright, Design and Patents Act 1988.

ISBN: 978-1-9995333-8-0

All rights reserved. No part of this publication may be reproduced, stored in a retrieval system, or transmitted, in any form or by any means, electronic, mechanical, photocopying, recording or otherwise, for public or private use – other than as brief quotations embodied in articles and reviews - without the prior consent of the author. This book is sold subject to the condition that it shall not, by way of trade or otherwise, be lent, resold, or hired out or otherwise circulated without the author's prior consent in any form of binding or cover other than that in which it is published.

The author's intent is only to offer entertainment and education for kids. The reader is solely responsible for their actions and results.

www.northstarsuccess.com
support@northstarsuccess.com

Bears are here, **bears** are there!
Bears are almost everywhere!
8 types of **bears** all over the world
From places warm to places cold
Bears are cute, **bears** are strong
Bears are predators all along

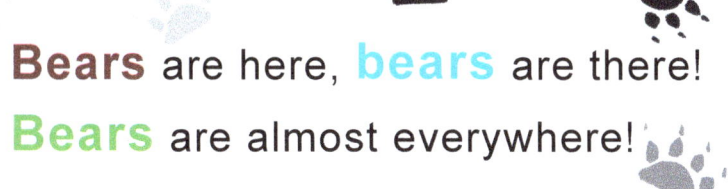

Bears have special powers
Not usual but superpowers
They climb up trees
They swim in the seas
They smell things like a dog
They run fast in the fog

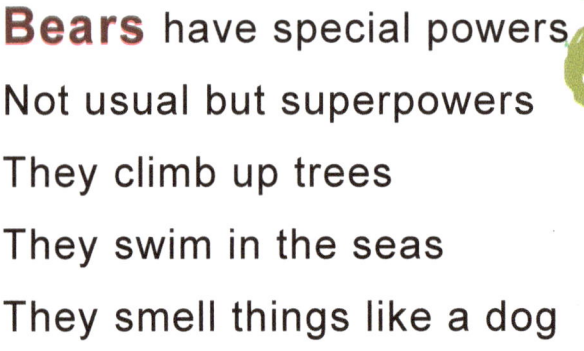

They hibernate when winter's around
In their cozy dens safe and sound
Bear Cubs are eager to learn
They follow their mother wherever she turns

We love animals big and small
Our favorite are bears above all

Bear Types around the World

There are 8 types of bears all around the world.

Black Bears, Brown Bears, Polar Bears, Andean Bears, Asiatic Black Bears, Panda Bears, Sloth Bears, and Sun Bears. Atlas Bears once lived in Africa but they are now extinct.

There are no bears in Australia except for zoos. Koalas are not bears in fact.

Hungry as a Bear

Bears are the largest predators and they spend up to 16 hours a day when they are not hibernating to look for food. They are greedy eaters. They actually build up the fat for their hibernation.

Symbols of Power, Intelligence and Love

Bears have large brains, good navigation skills, excellent smelling, sight and hearing. They care about their cubs and grieve for others. They actually even give bear hugs to each other and of course not us!

Playful Bear Cubs

Bear Cubs are born from mother bears in dens in winter. They are born blind and helpless. They stay with their mothers for 2 years to learn everything they need and be protected.

Now to have some bear fun, cut the bear masks and claws, and stick them on a cardboard paper. Attach a plastic rubber to the sides and enjoy the endless possibilities of joy!

North American Black Bear

Brown Bear

Polar Bear

Andean Bear

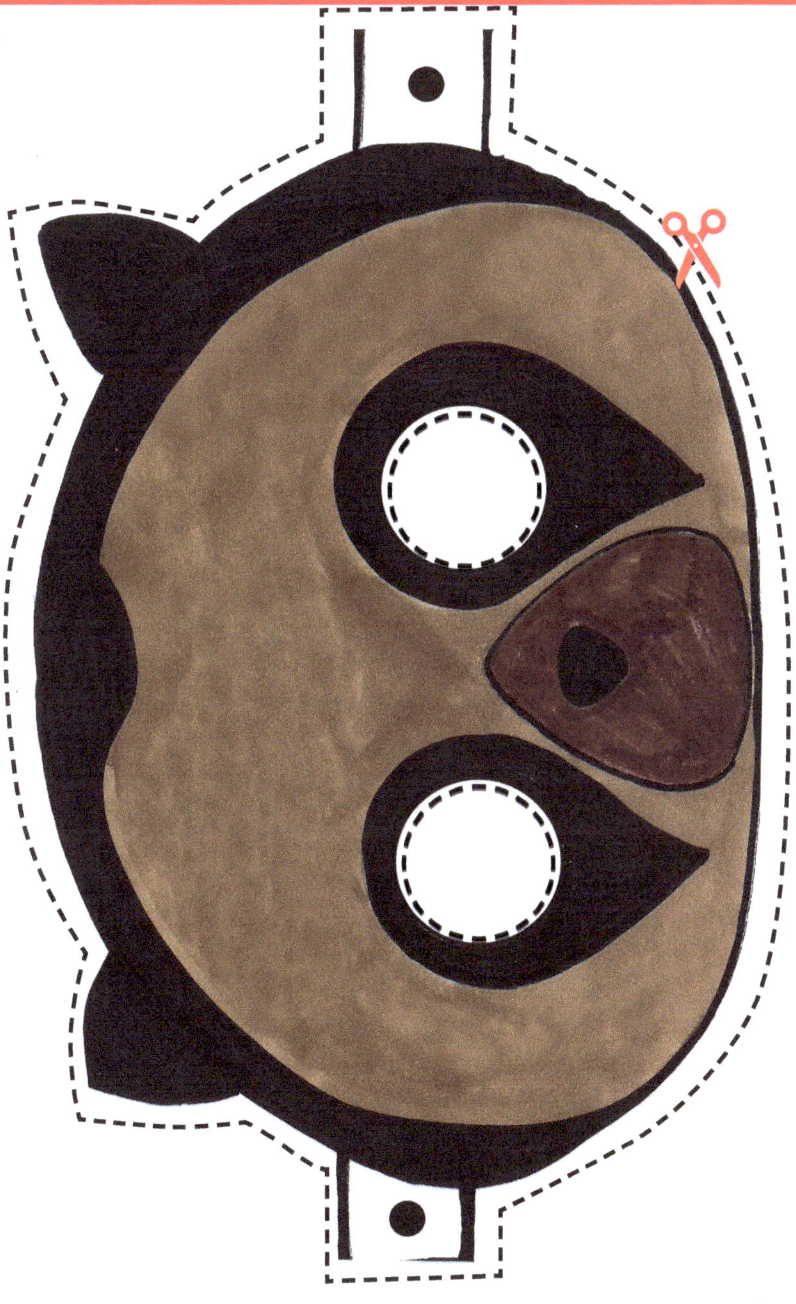

Asiatic Black Bear

Panda Bear

Sloth Bear

Sun Bear

Atlas Bear

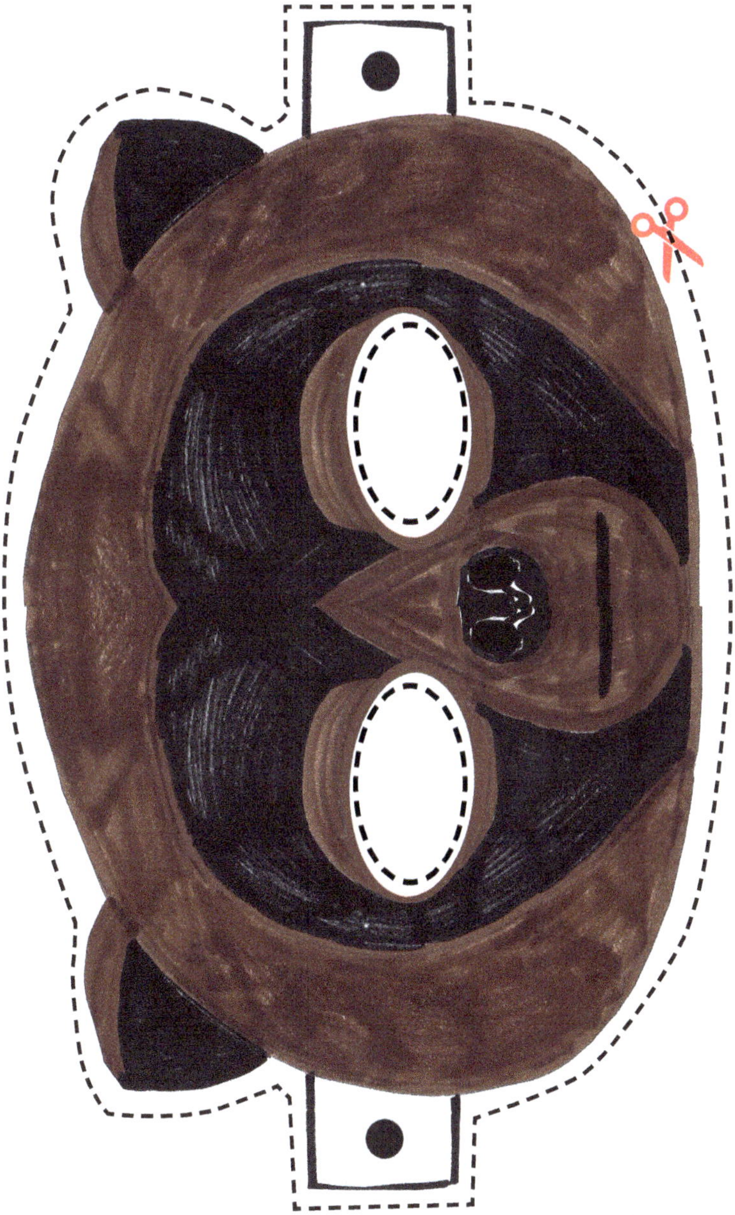

Claws

References:

https://bearwithus.org/

https://en.wikipedia.org/wiki/Atlas_bear

https://onekindplanet.org/animal/bear/

www.ingramcontent.com/pod-product-compliance
Lightning Source LLC
Chambersburg PA
CBHW061204070526
44579CB00010B/125